Peggy Louise Parrish
Parma, Idaho
Cover Pictures by Peggy Louise Parrish
Interior Artwork by Peggy Louise Parrish

ISBN-13; 978-1542871181
Printed in The United States of America

The Classy Letter C

Coloring Book

By Peggy Louise Parrish

c. 2017

Welcome to the Classy Letter C

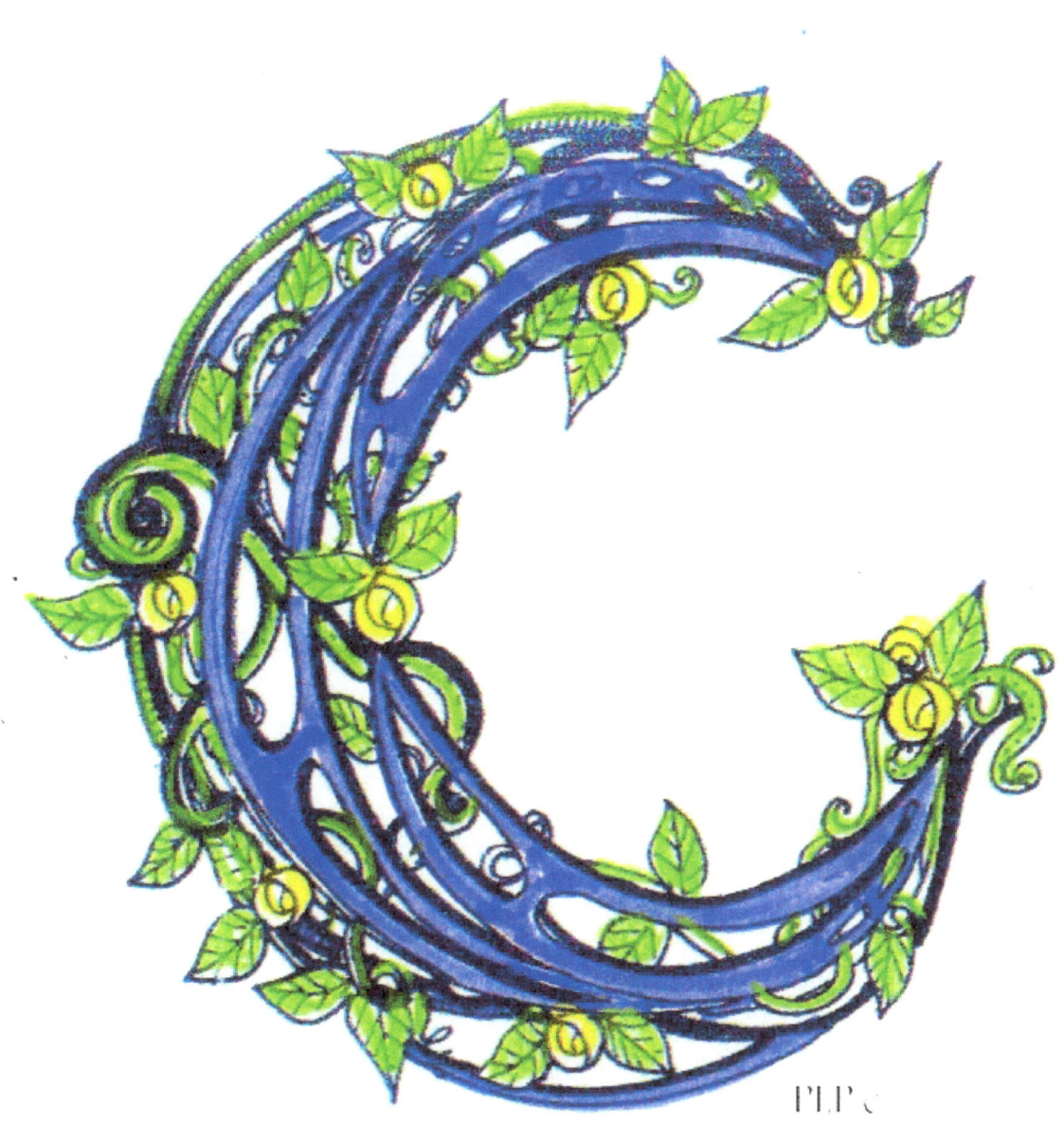

Letter C is so fun to color in

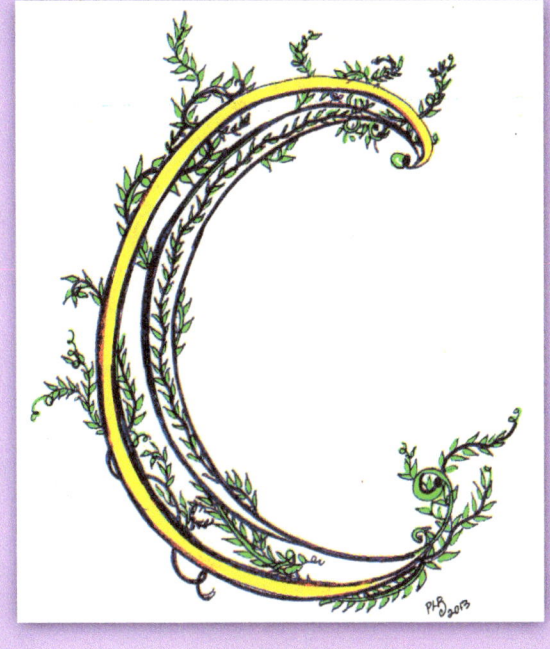

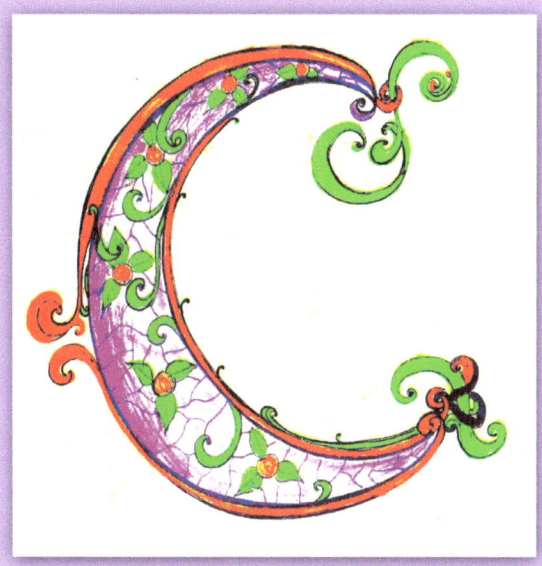

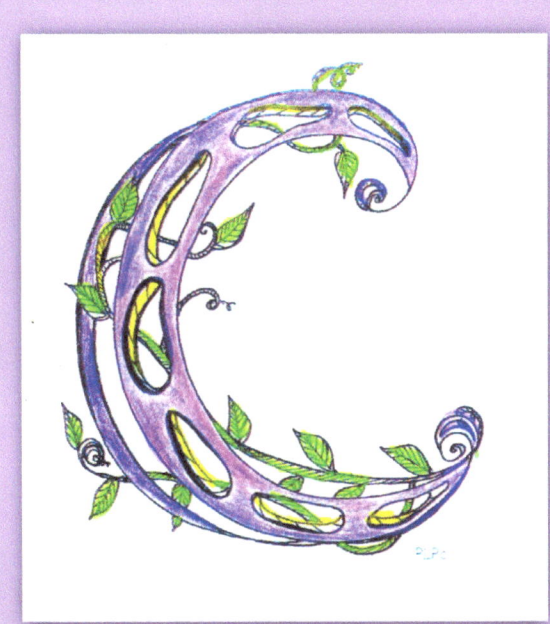

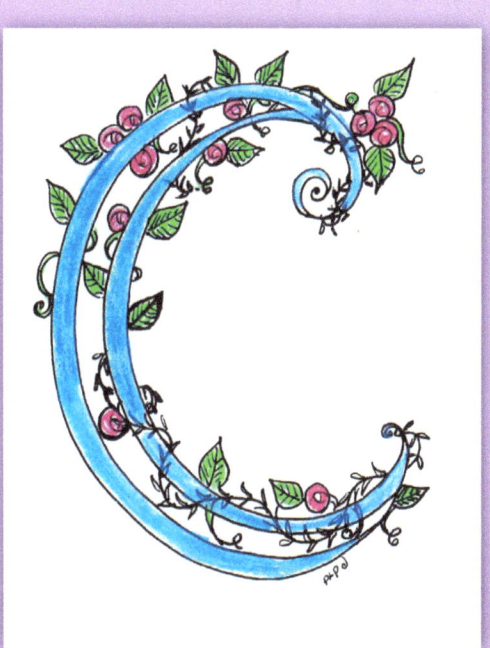

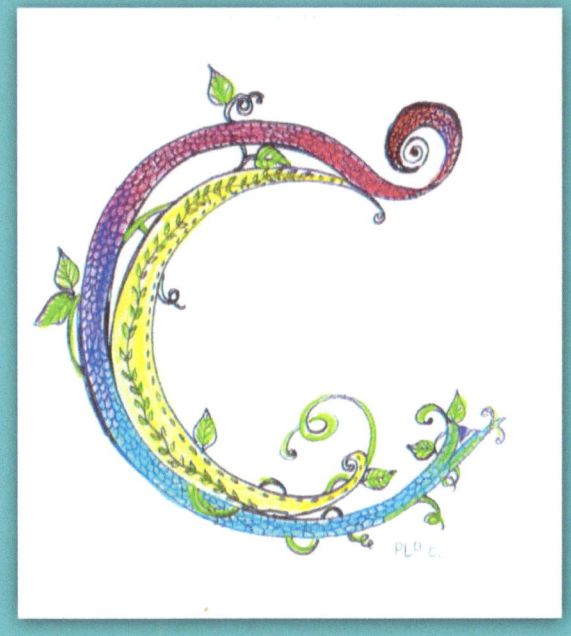

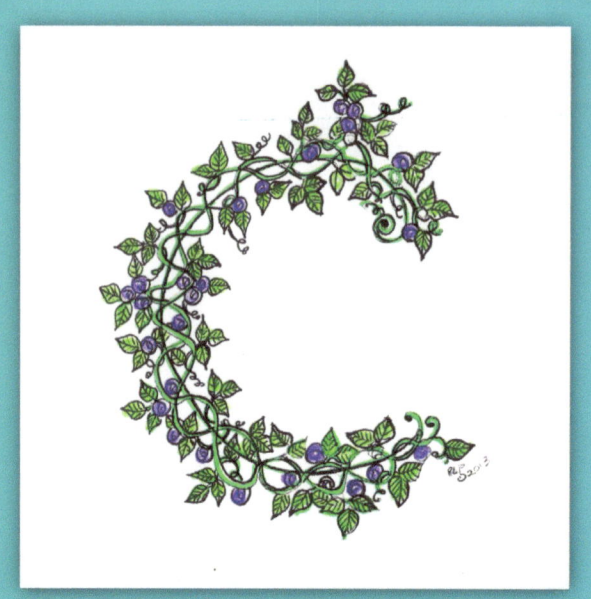

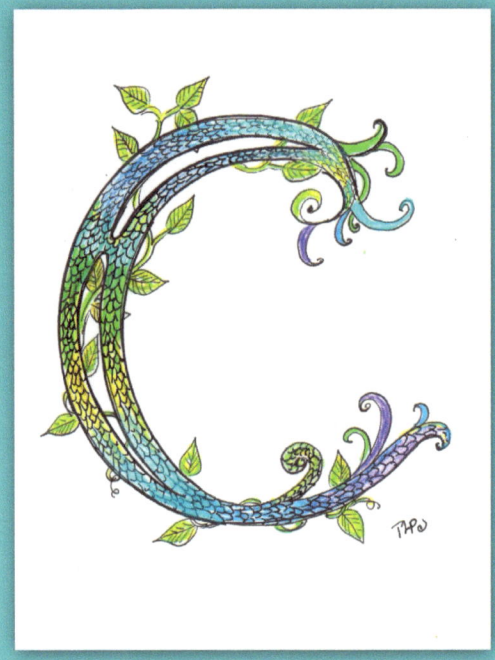

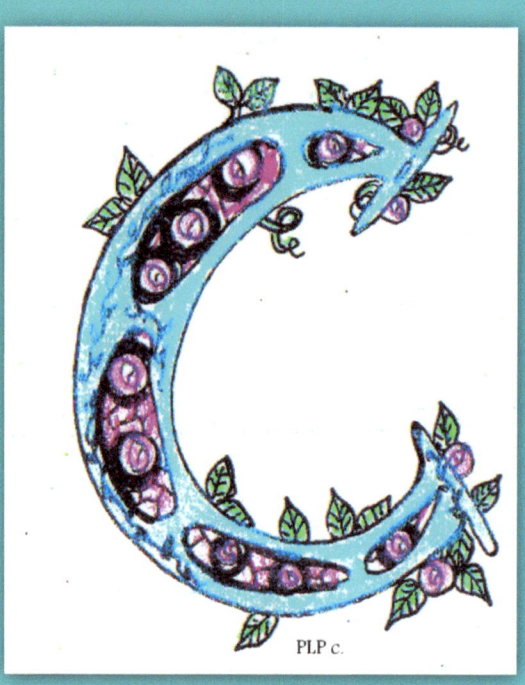

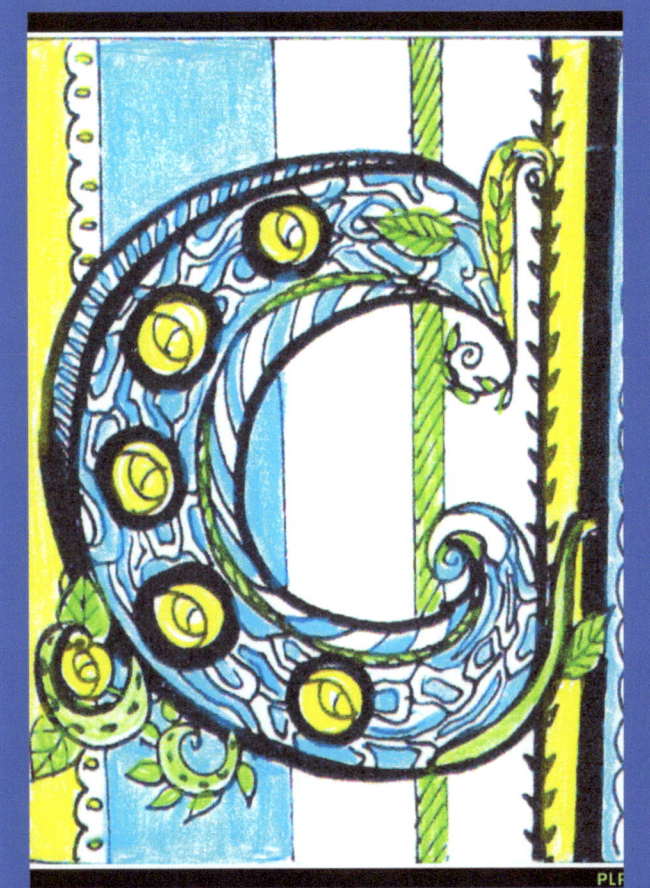

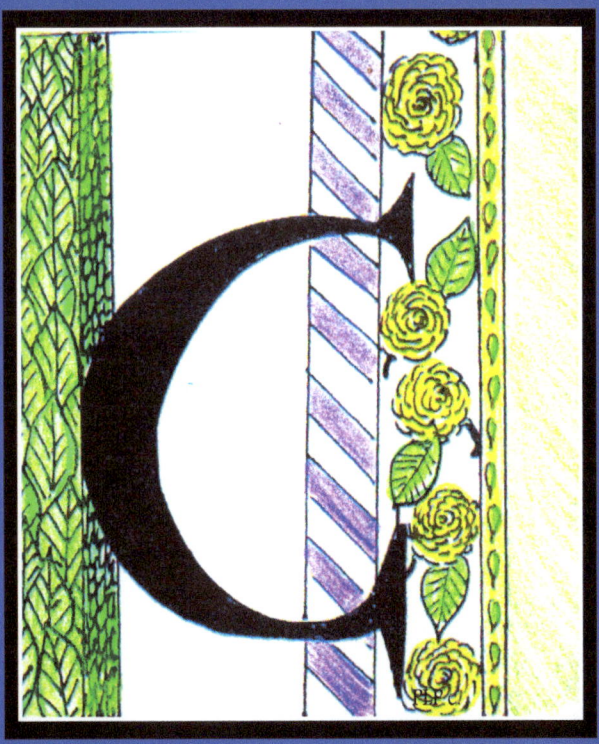
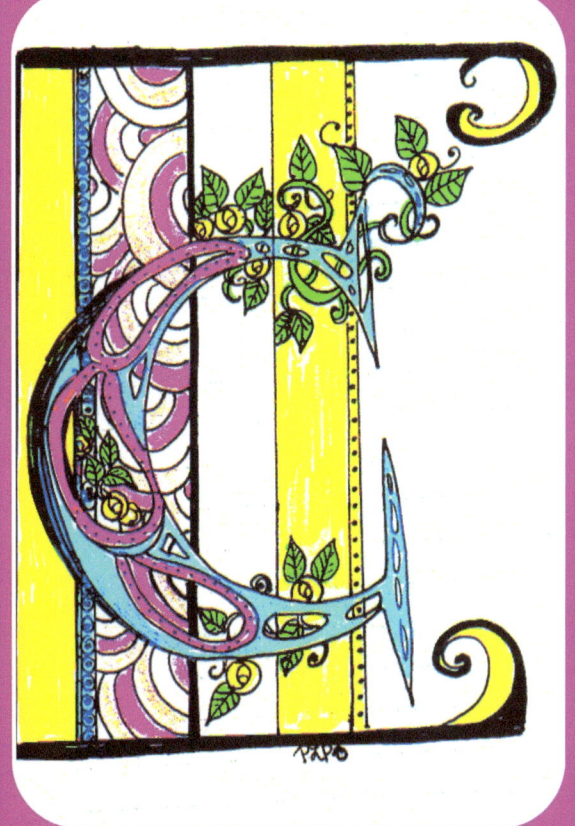

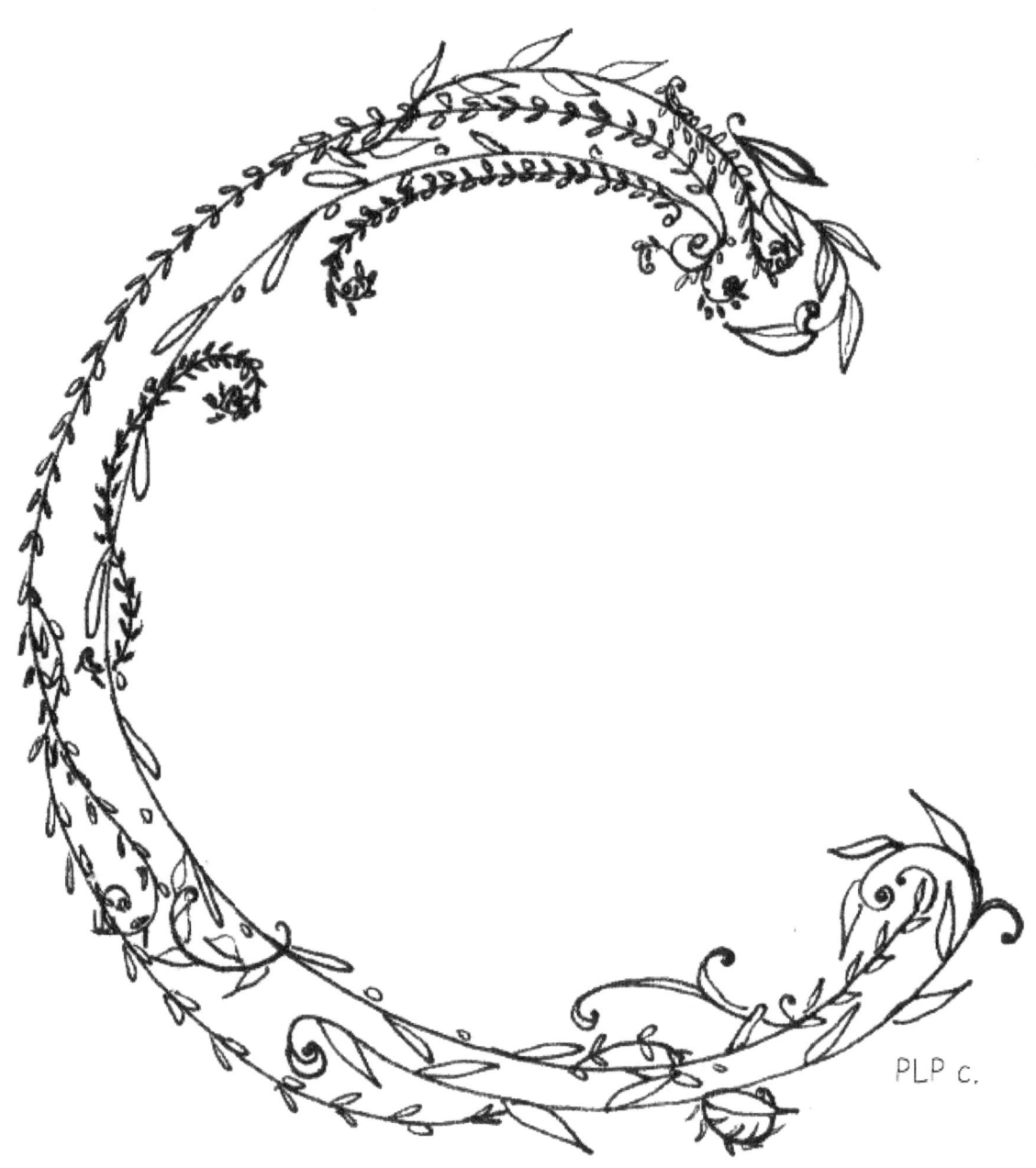

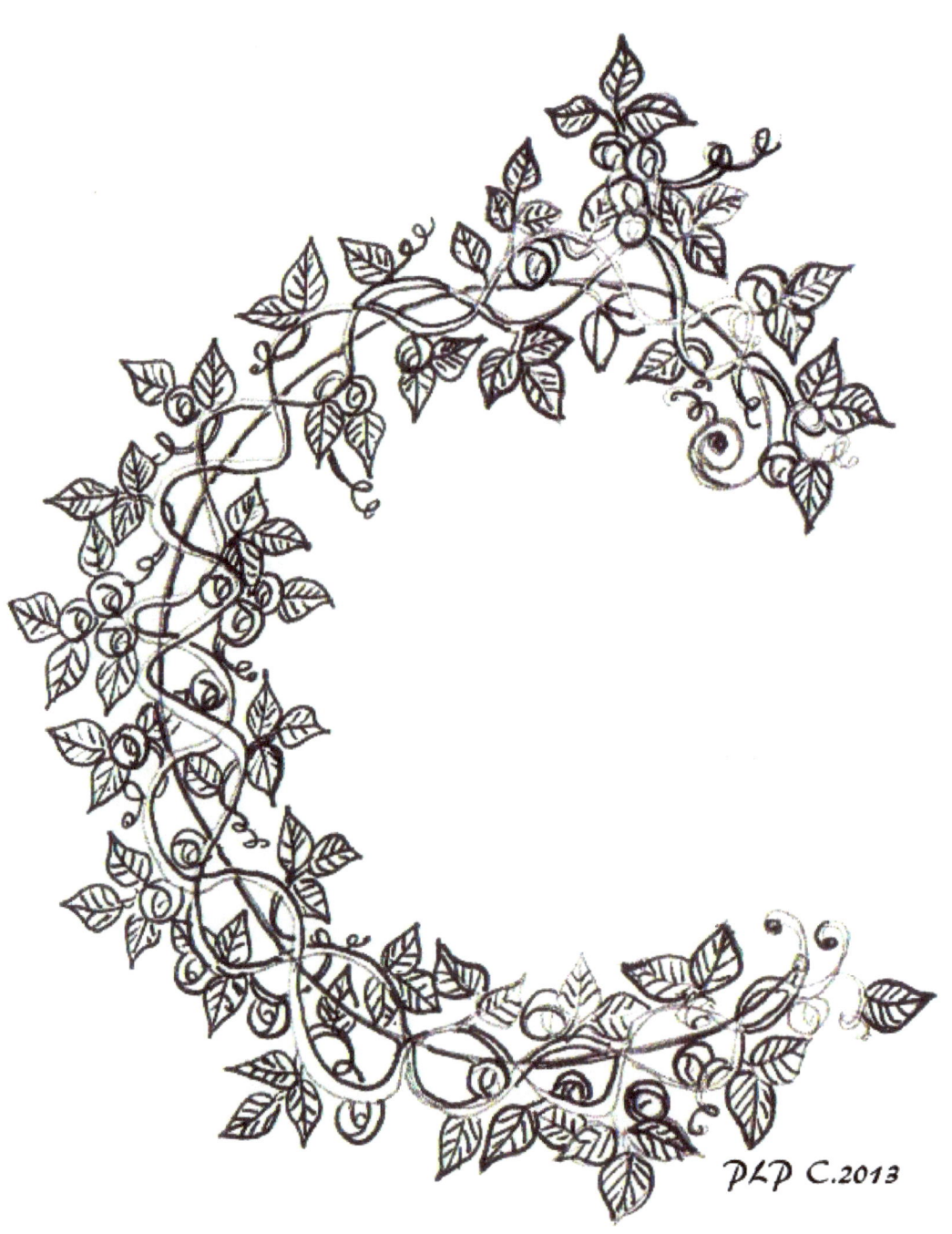

PLP C.2013

13

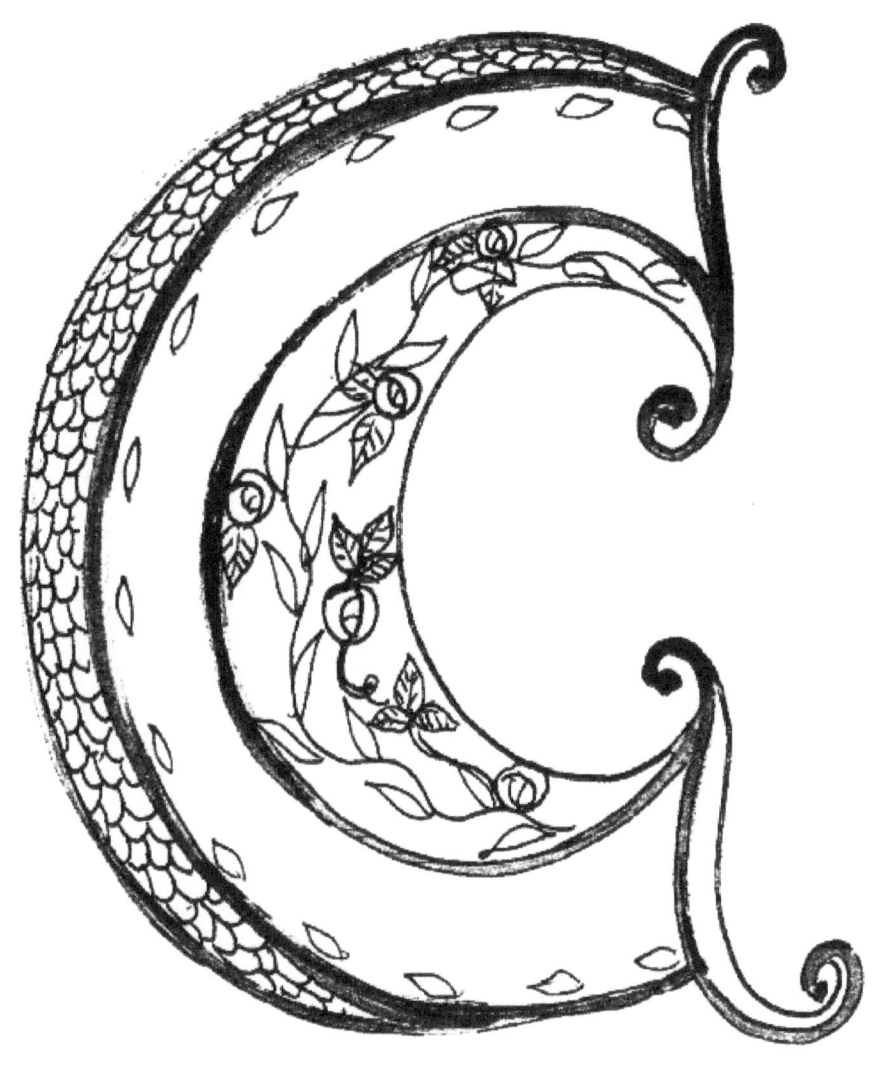

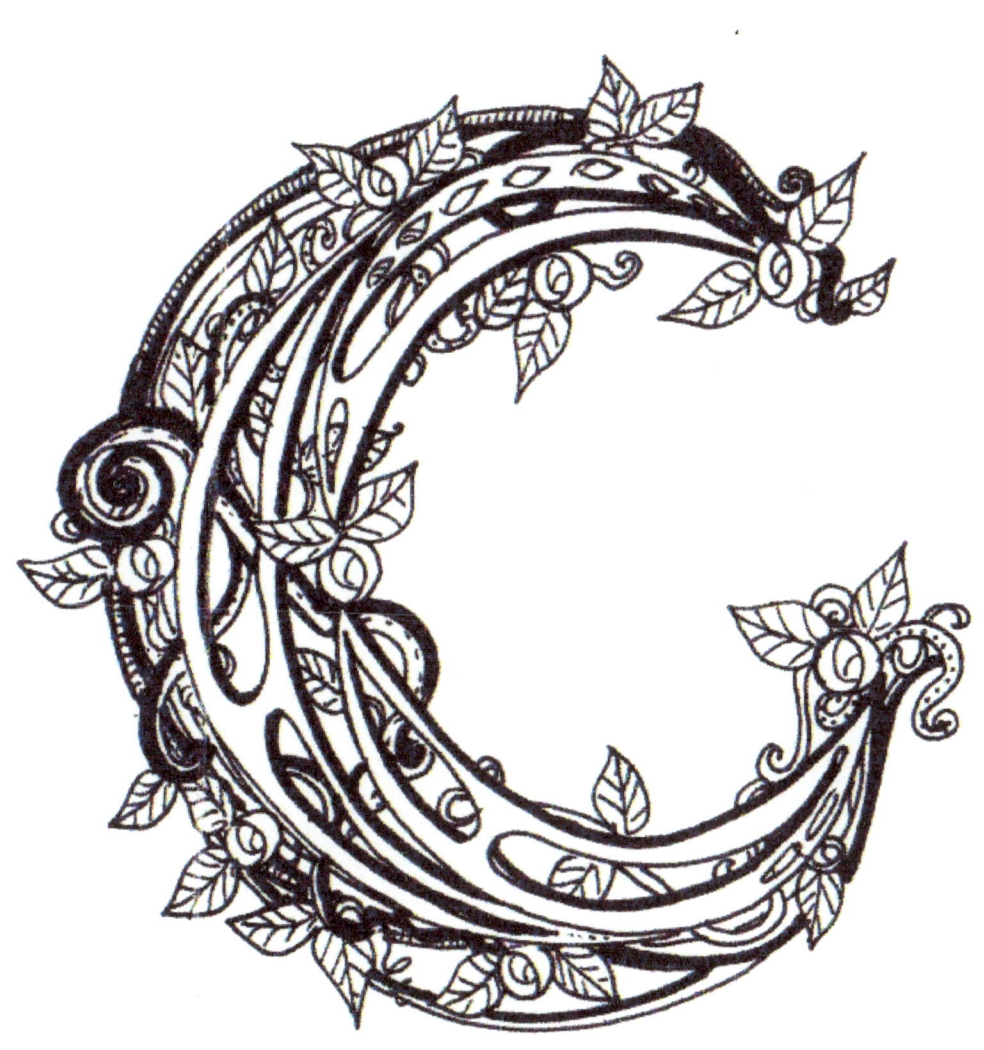

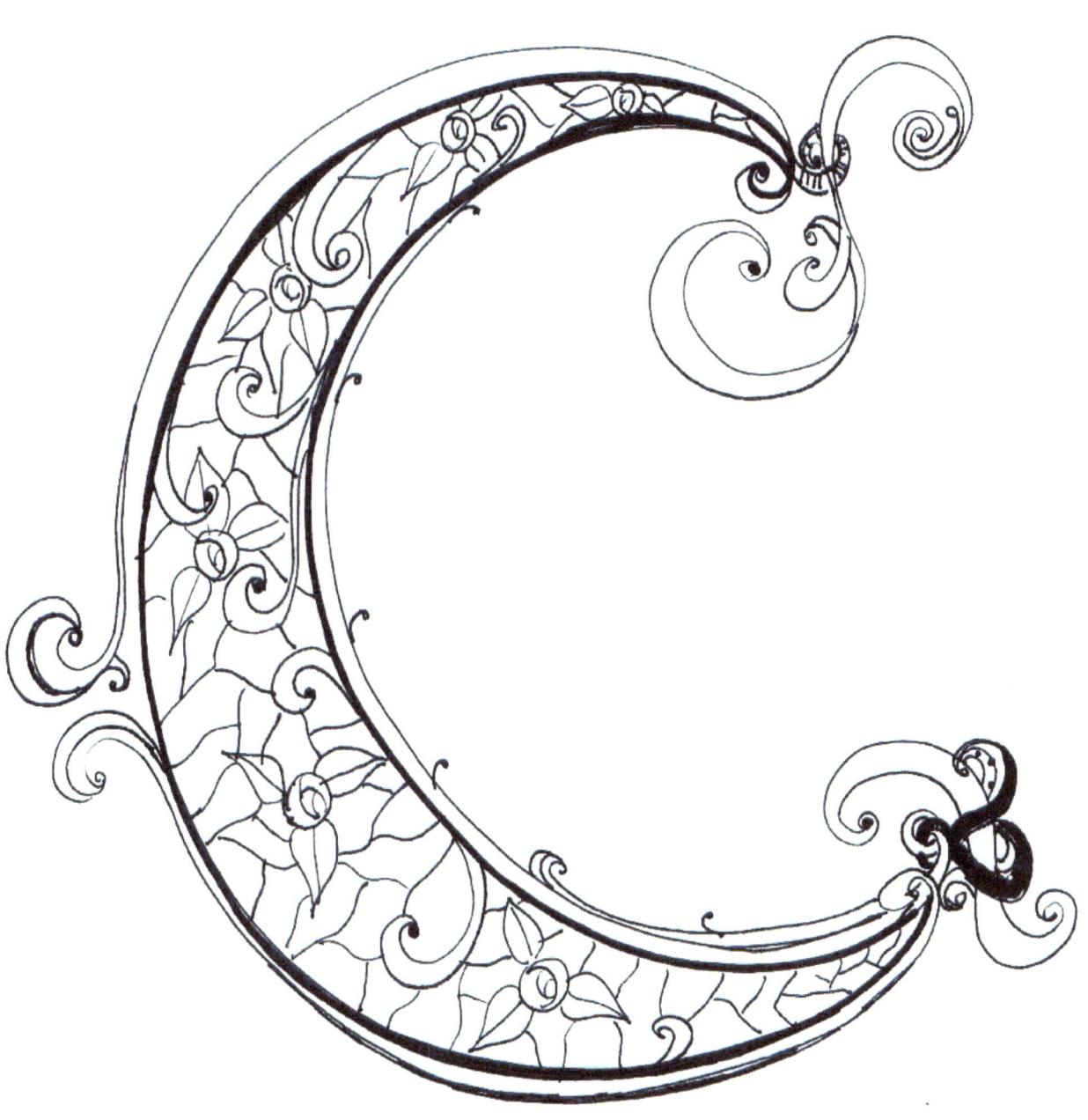

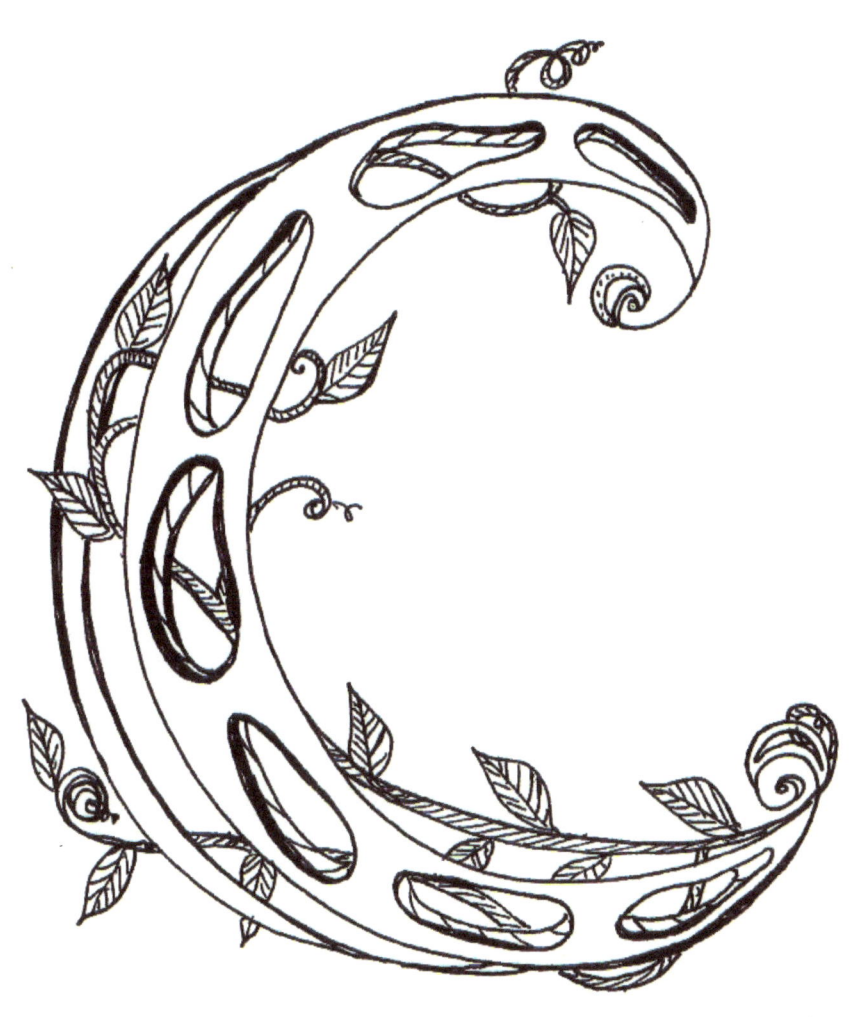

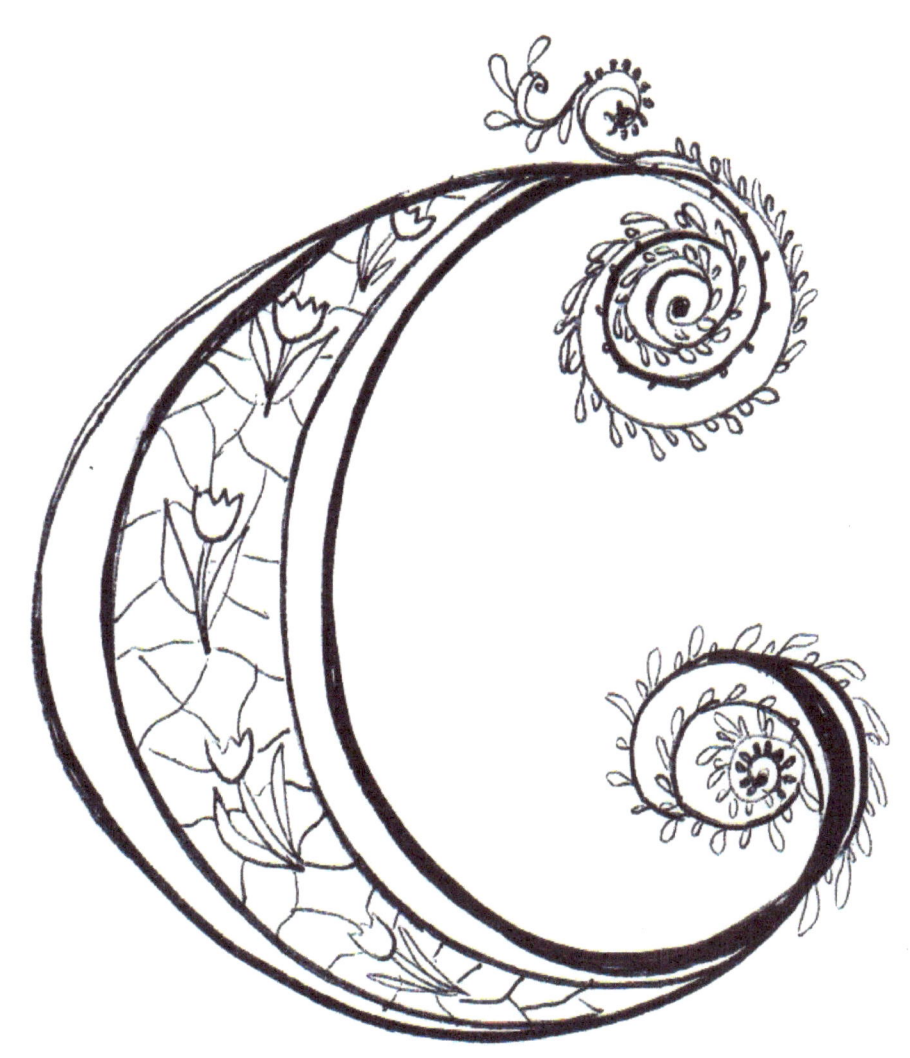

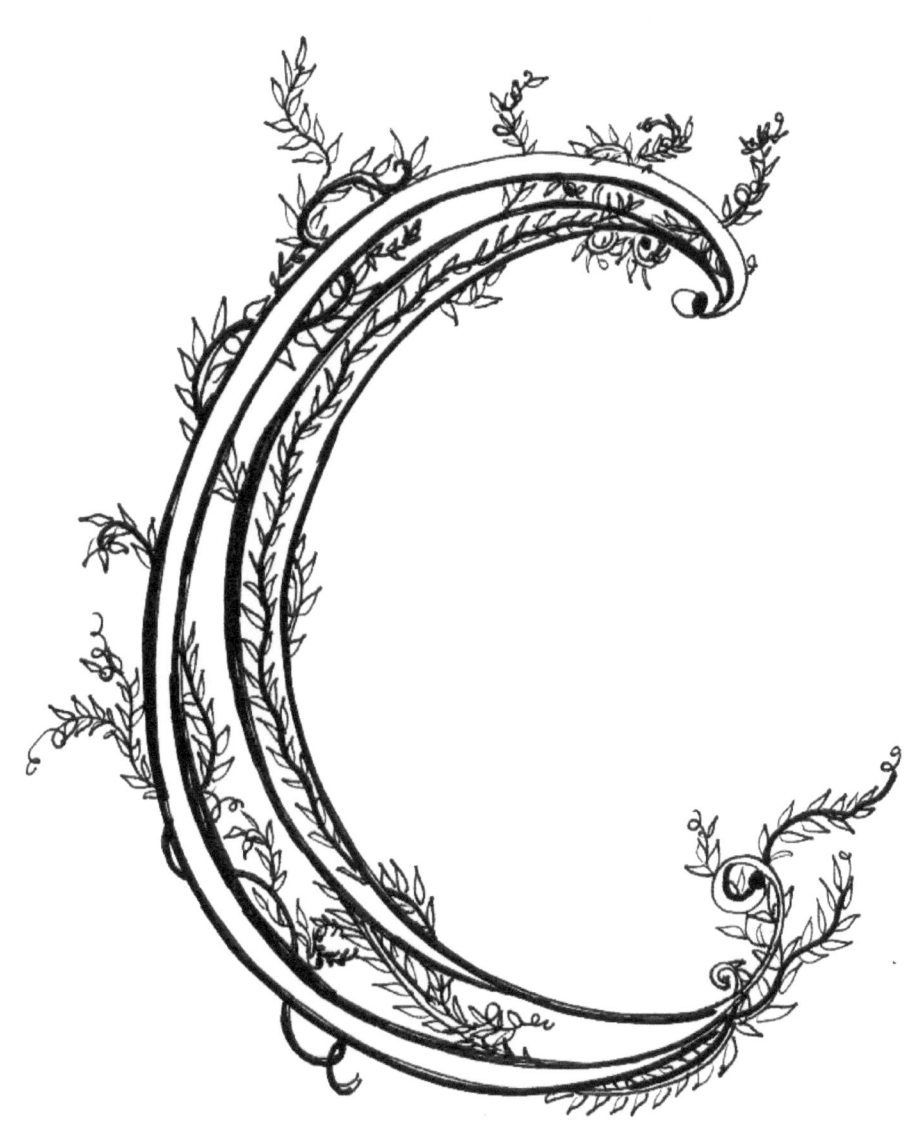

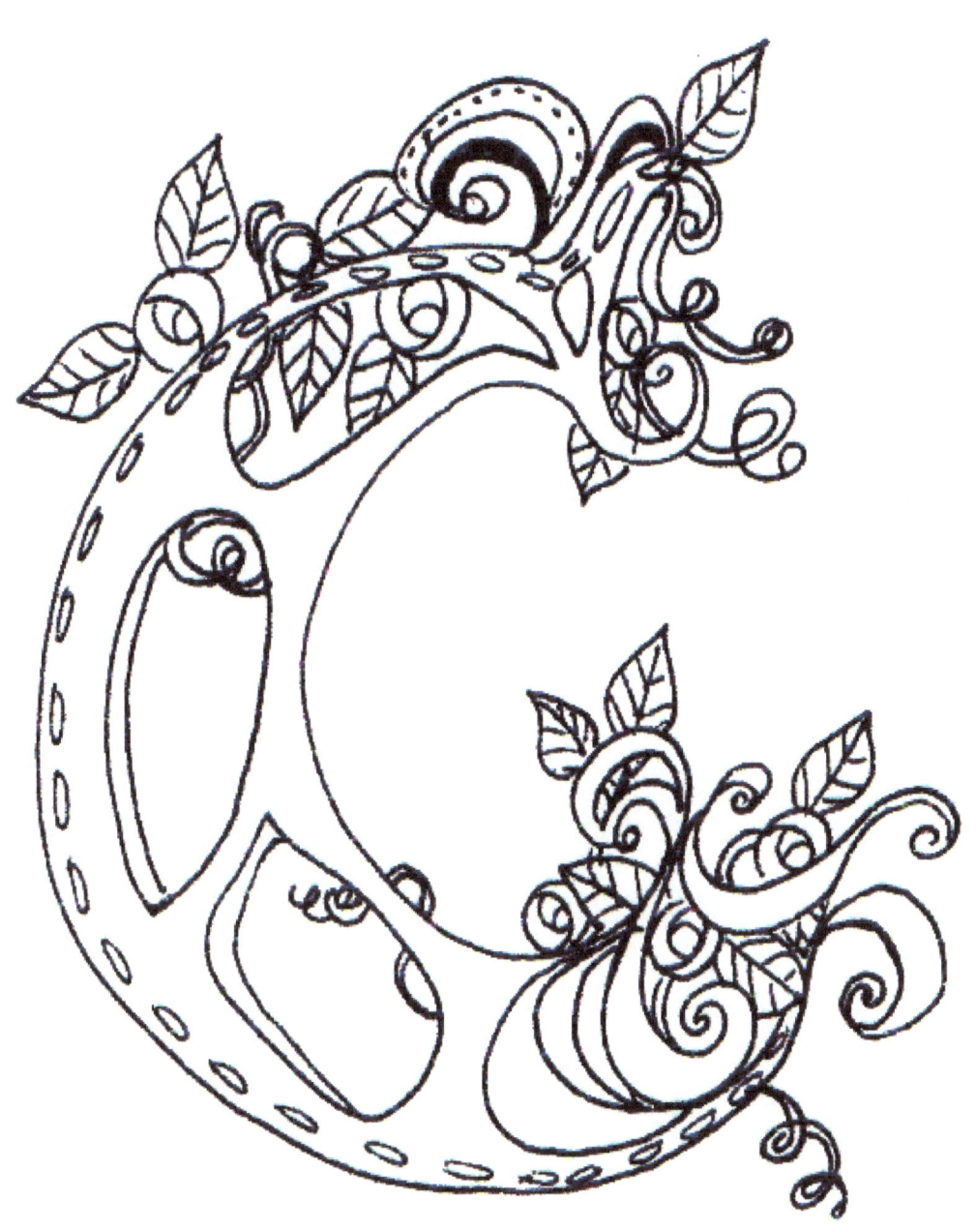

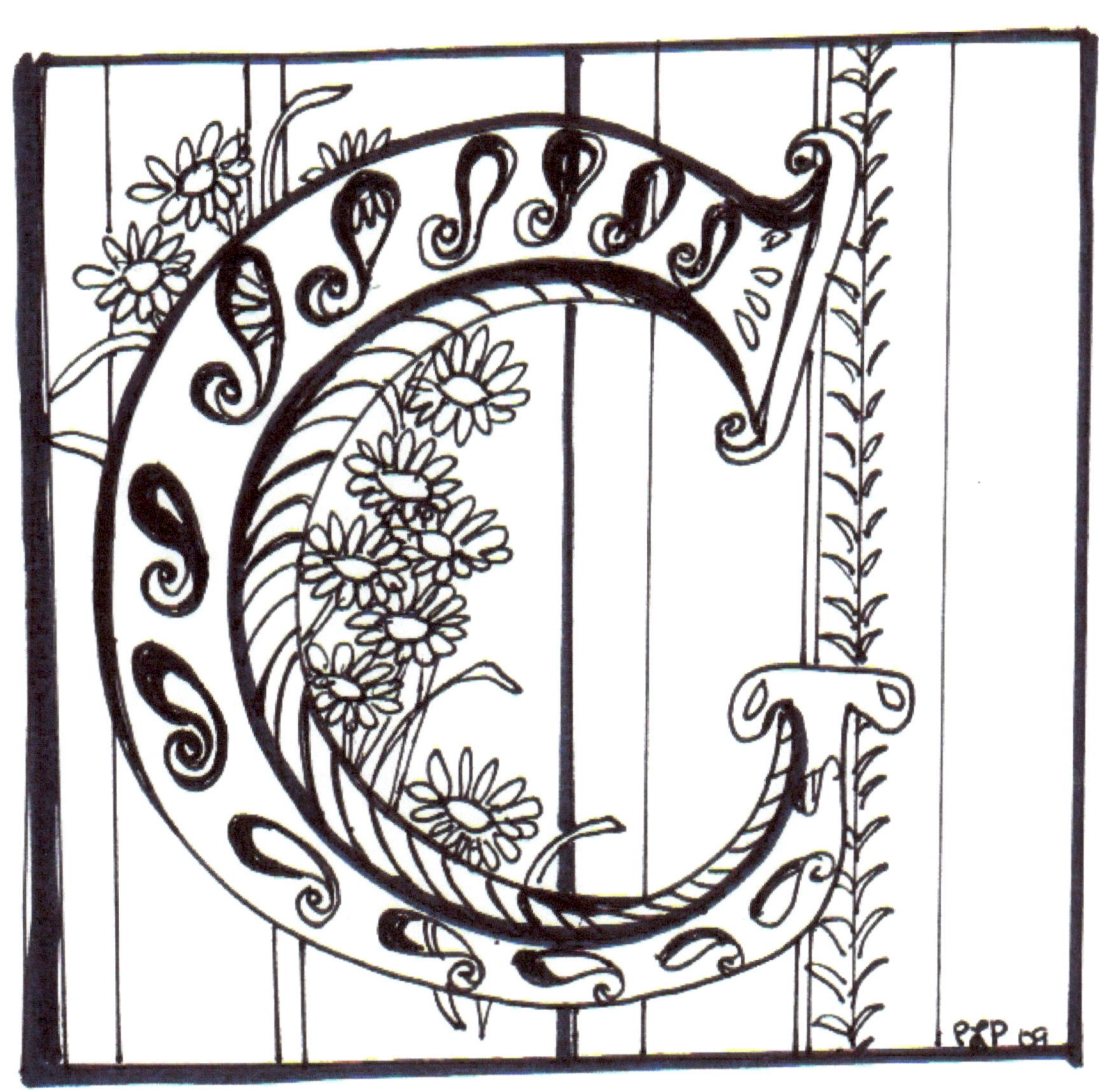

29

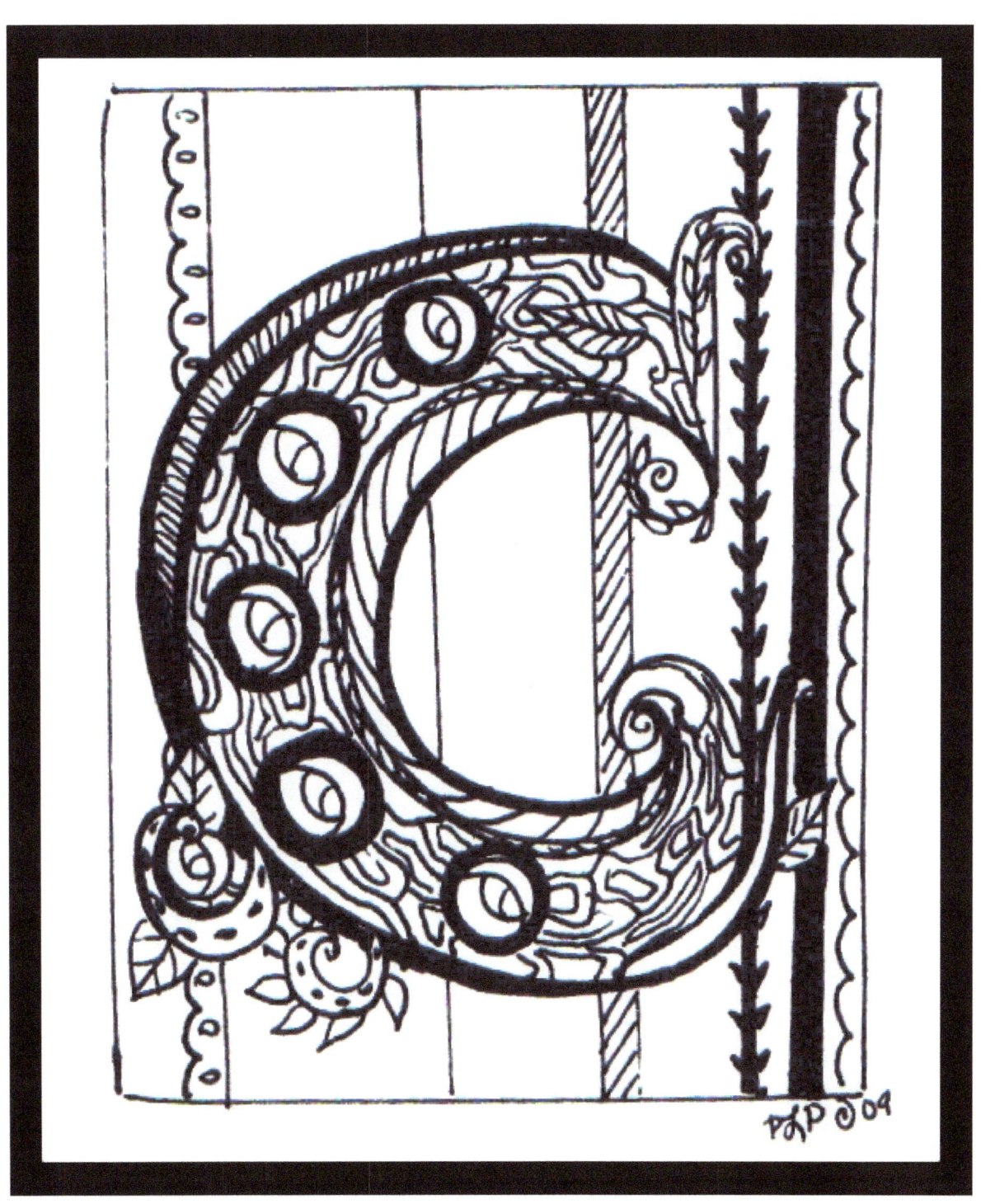

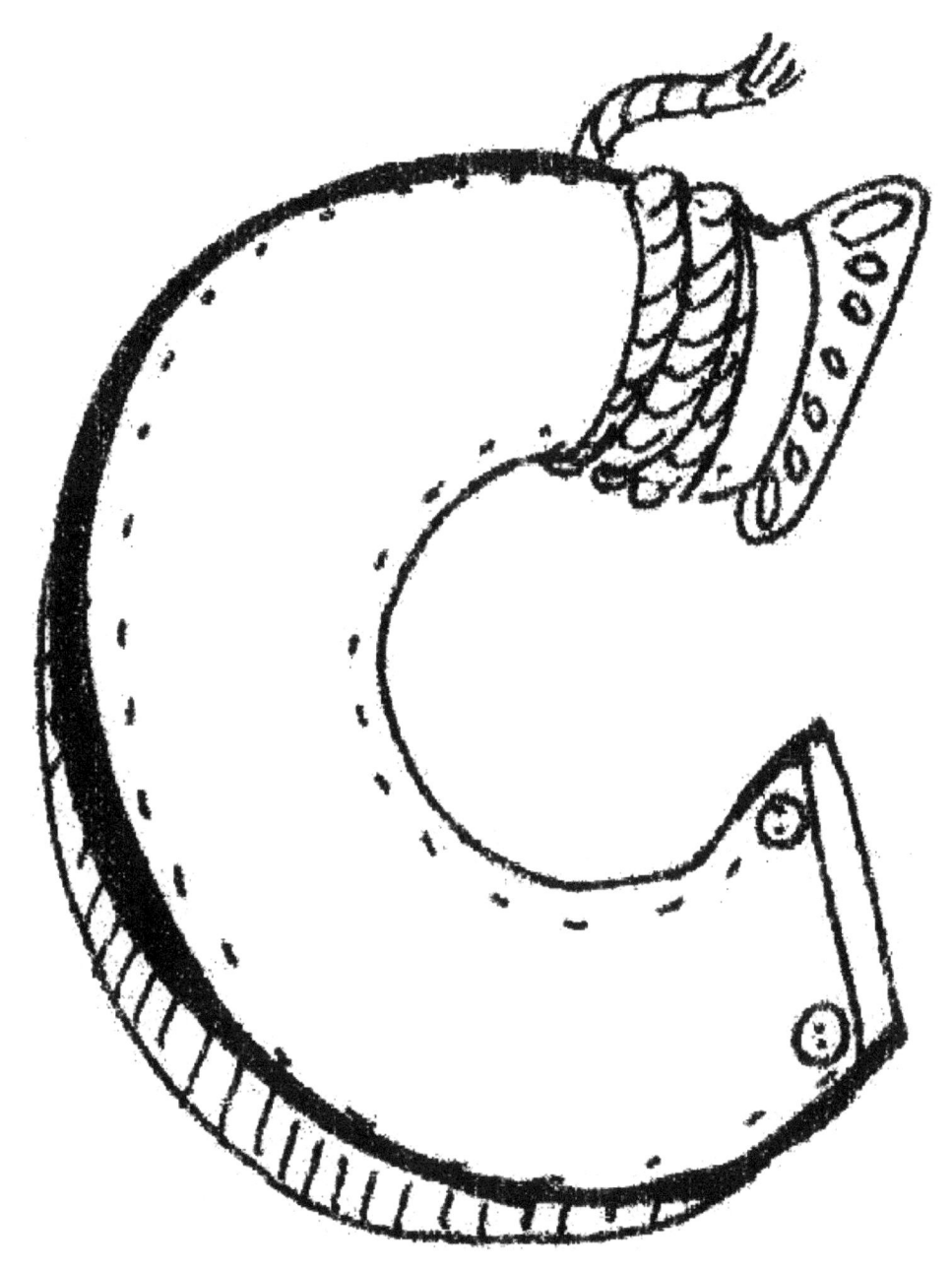

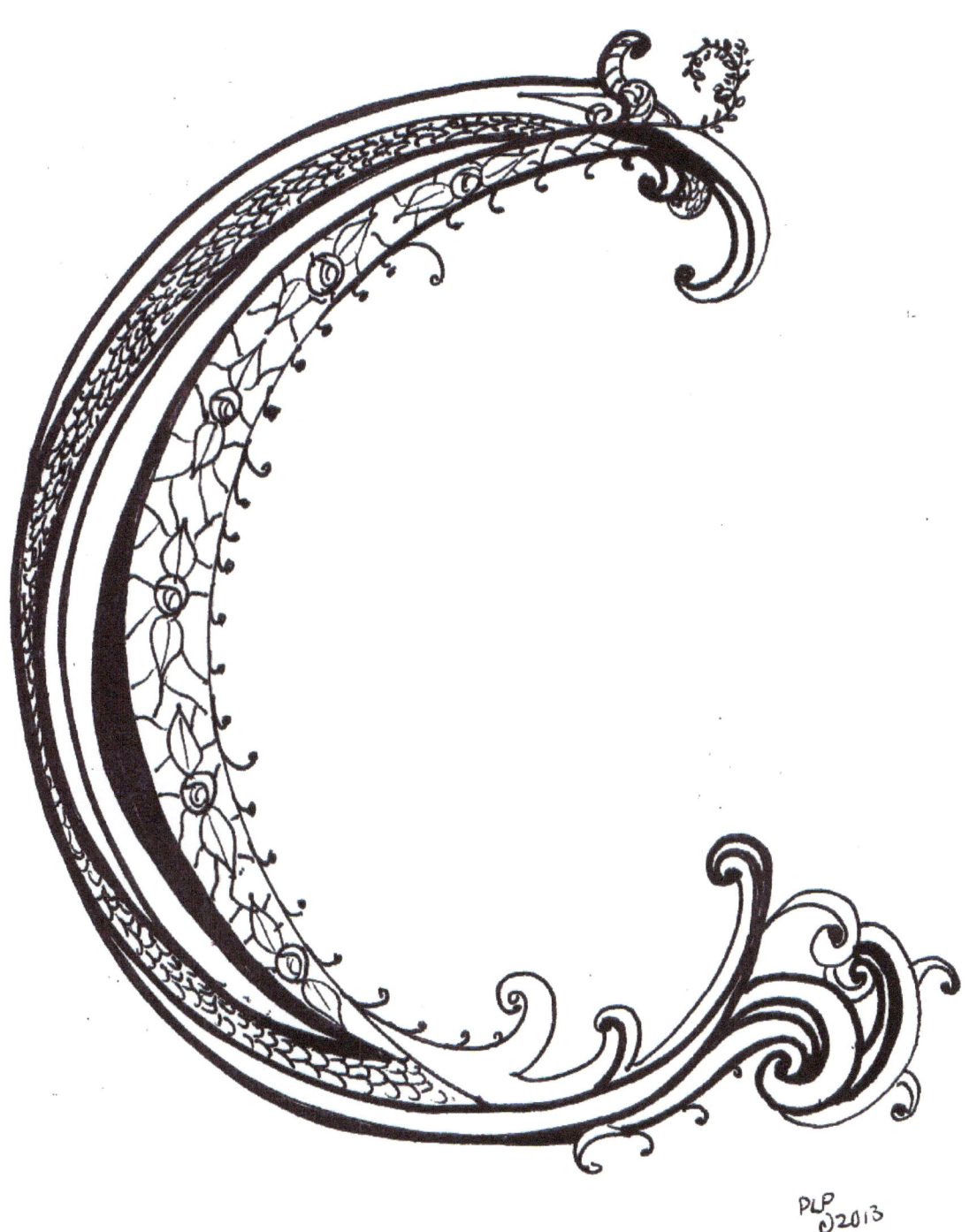

PLP
2013

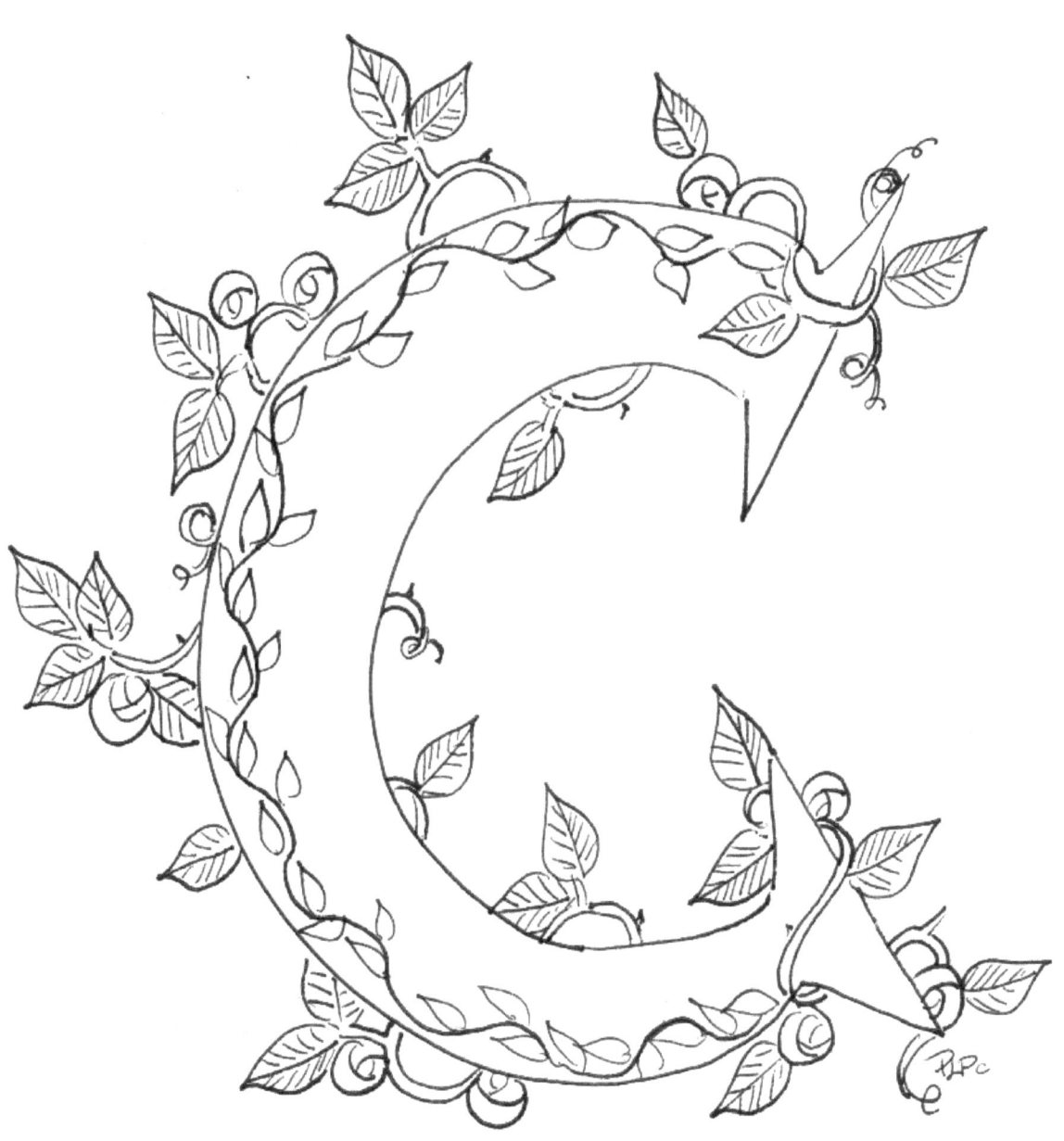

PLP c.

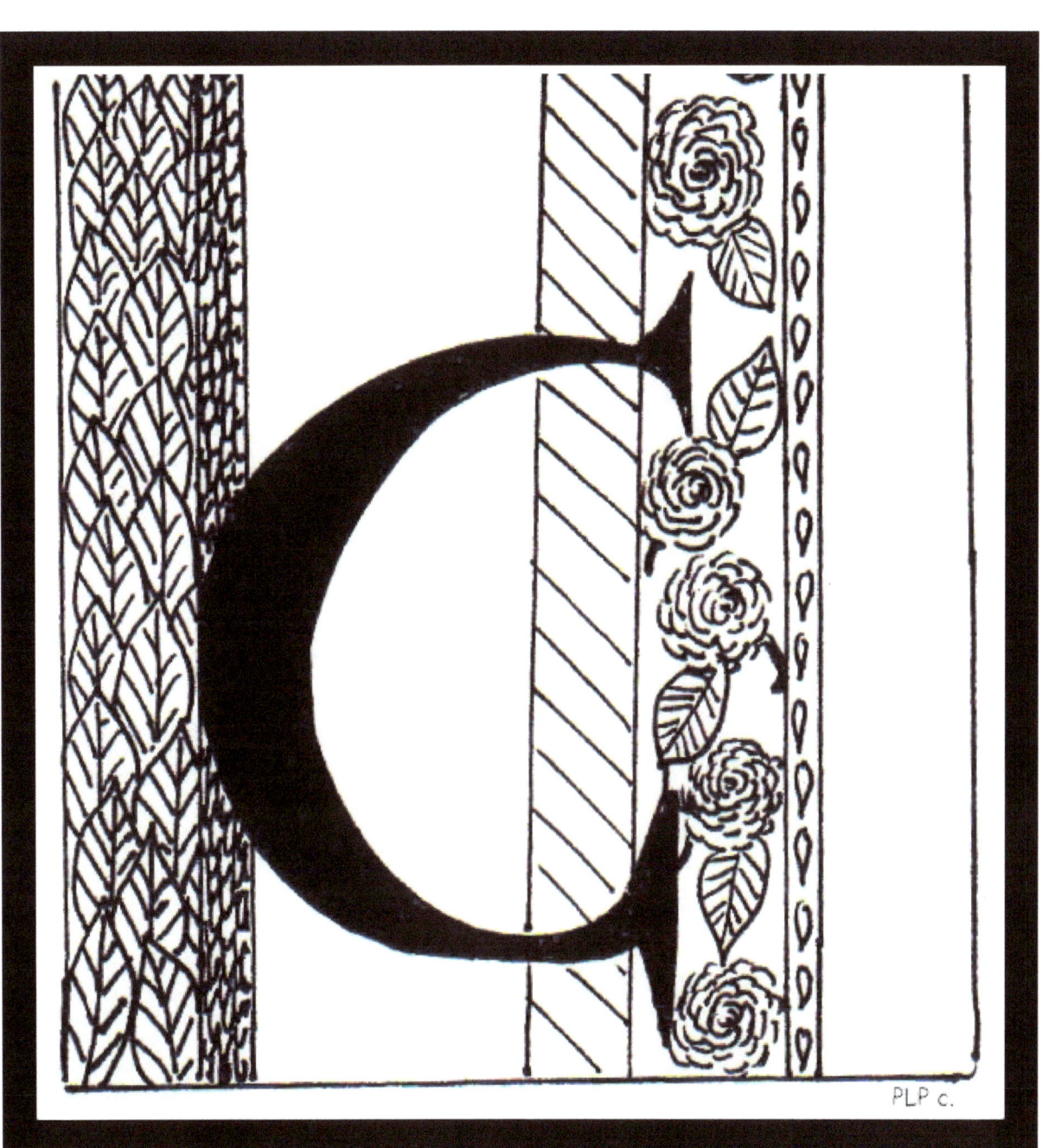

PLP c.

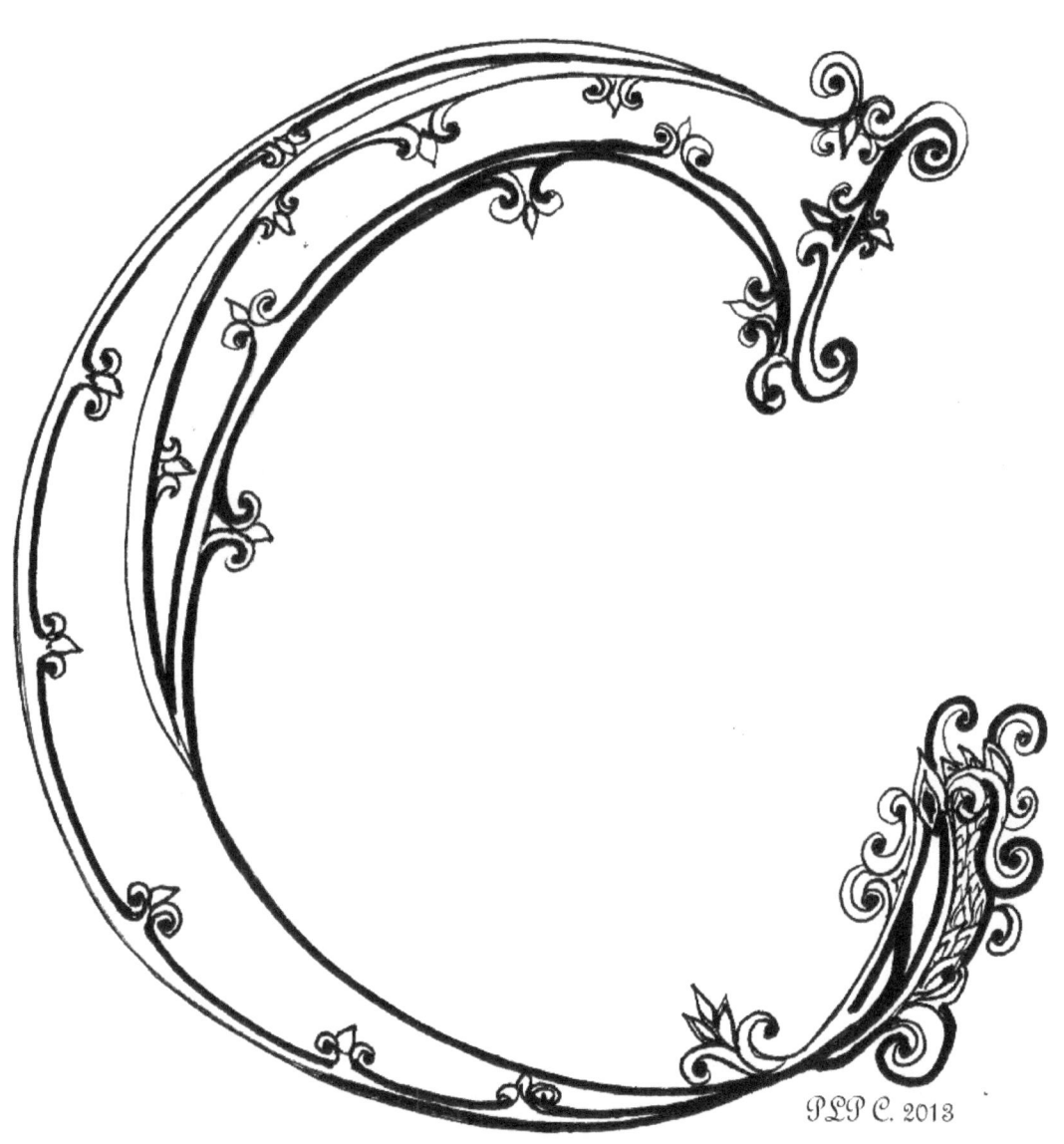

PLP C. 2013

Here's a fun thing to try.

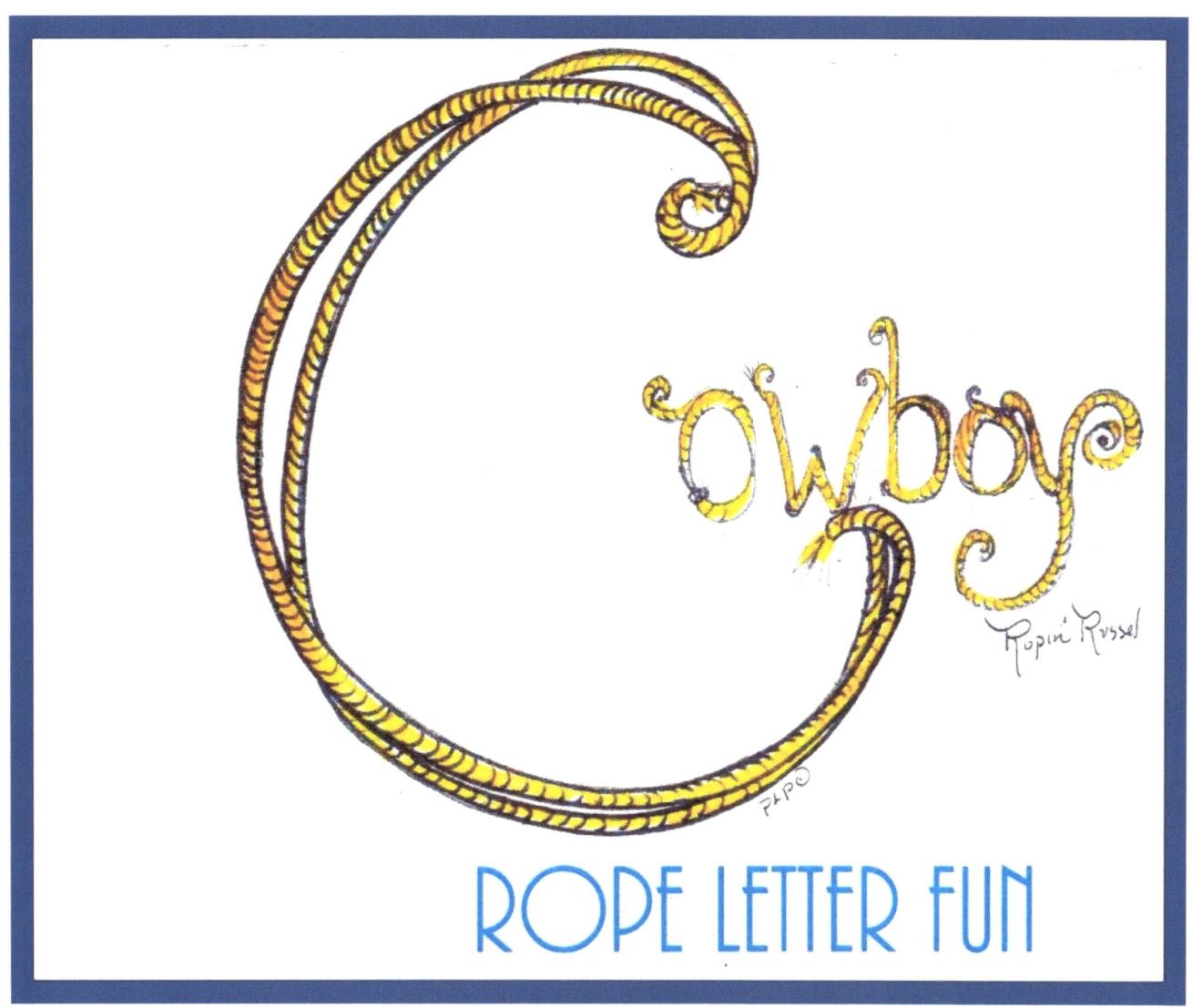

ROPE LETTER FUN

A CLASSY COWBOY C

Here is a fun way to use a hand designed bandana letter C

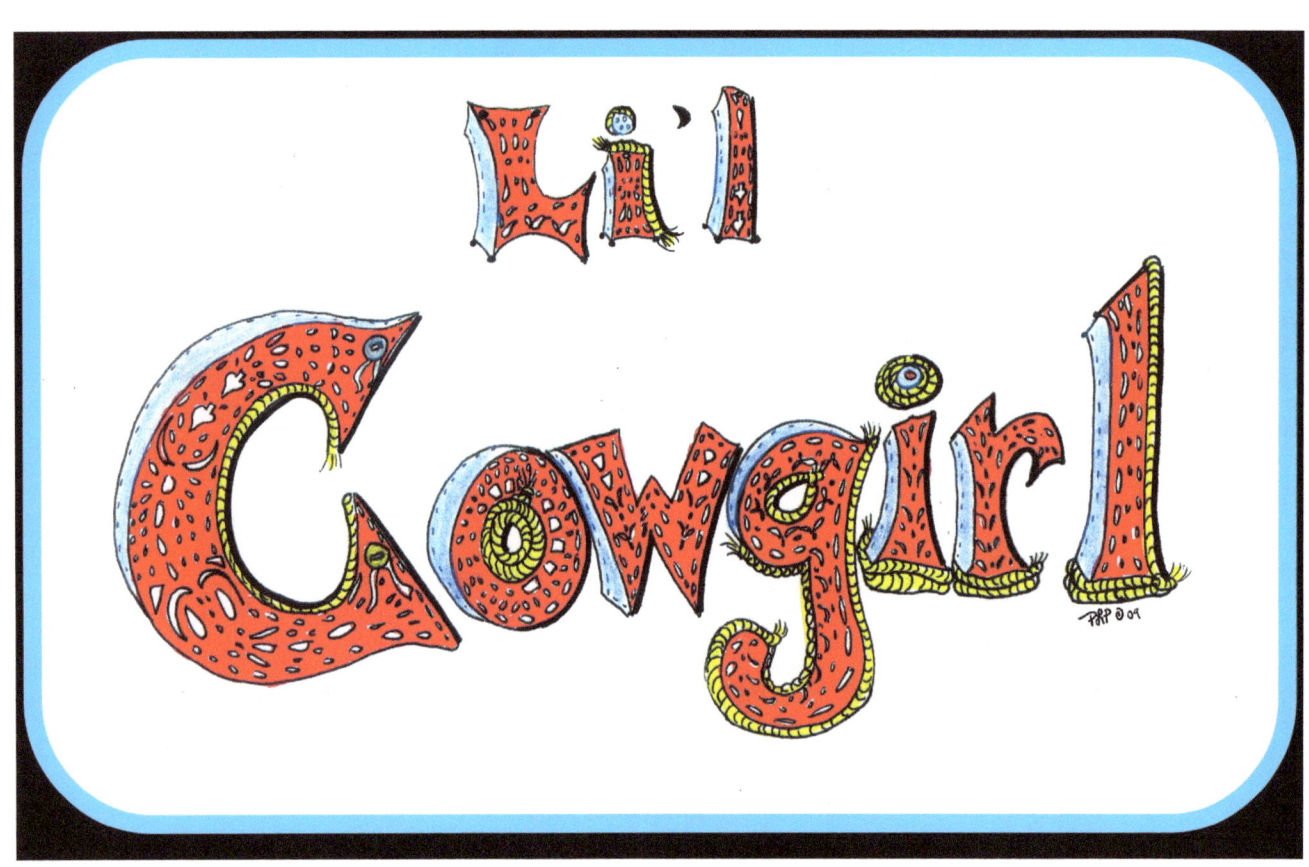

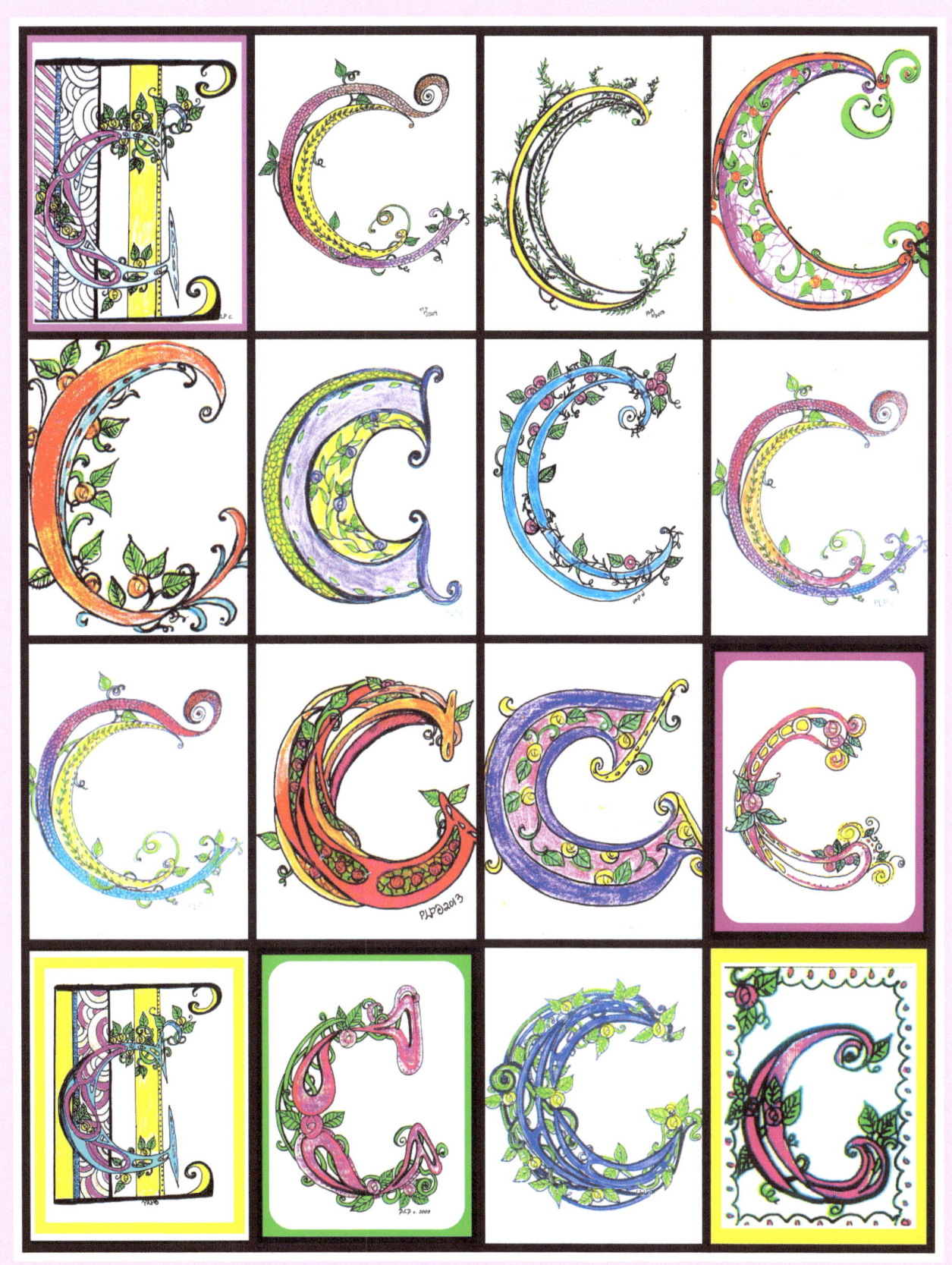

Don't forget to visit our other letter book. You might want to tackle the whole alphabet with COLOR. Coloring things anyway you feel like it is a great therapy for any one.

Or if you are really inspired by this book make some C letters up yourself! Then color them.

www.ingramcontent.com/pod-product-compliance
Lightning Source LLC
Chambersburg PA
CBHW051059180526
45172CB00002B/706